ANGEL Gabriel SPEAKS

MARIE-JOSÉE THIBAULT

Angel Gabriel Speaks: Book 1
Published by Abba Books LLC
abbabooksllc@gmail.com
Copyright © 2023 Marie-Josée Thibault

All Rights Reserved

No part of this publication may be reproduced, distributed, or transmitted in any form or by any means, including photocopying, recording, or other electronic or mechanical methods, without the prior written permission of the publisher.

First Edition, 2023
Designed and Edited by Abba Books LLC
ISBN: 979-8-9875984-2-9

Abba Books LLC
34972 Newark Blvd, #441
Newark, CA 94560

www.abbamyfatheriloveyou.com
https://www.facebook.com/AbbaILoveYouBooks/

CONTENTS

PREFACE	VII	Chapter 11	21
Chapter 1	1	Chapter 12	23
Chapter 2	3	Chapter 13	25
Chapter 3	5	Chapter 14	27
Chapter 4	7	Chapter 15	29
Chapter 5	9	Chapter 16	31
Chapter 6	11	Chapter 17	33
Chapter 7	13	Chapter 18	35
Chapter 8	15	Chapter 19	37
Chapter 9	17	Chapter 20	39
Chapter 10	19	Chapter 21	41

Chapter 22	43	Chapter 33	65
Chapter 23	45	Chapter 34	67
Chapter 24	47	Chapter 35	69
Chapter 25	49	Chapter 36	71
Chapter 26	51	Chapter 37	73
Chapter 27	53	Chapter 38	75
Chapter 28	55	Chapter 39	77
Chapter 29	57	Chapter 40	79
Chapter 30	59	Chapter 41	81
Chapter 31	61	Chapter 42	83
Chapter 32	63	Chapter 43	85

Angel Gabriel Speaks

Jibrīl

PREFACE

My dear friends of the whole Earth, listen attentively to the glorious and enlightened Words of Truth that Gabriel brings to all mankind. The Archangel Gabriel is magnificent! He has beautiful gold-colored hair, a silver armor, and a gentle, loving face. How beautiful He is! May the Angel Gabriel continue to visit the humans assigned to Him by Abba Father/Allah.

Gabriel, I love you!

Marie-Josée Thibault

FREE DOWNLOAD

Get your free copy of : "Dear Humanity: Book 1" when you sign up to the author's VIP mailing list! Get started here:

www.abbamyfatheriloveyou.com

CHAPTER 1

I, Gabriel, the Angel of the Lord, the Angel of Allah, have come down to visit Marie-Josée on Earth, the essence of Mohammed, peace be upon him.

I love you.

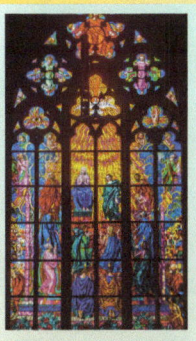

CHAPTER 2

I teach you today, through Marie-Josée on Earth, the essence of Mohammad, peace be upon him, about the army of Jesus who is already protecting you and who will protect you even more when the war is actively and ruthlessly in force.

The war to come, my children, will be the greatest and most terrible world war, which will destroy more than two-thirds of humanity. This war will announce the coming of Jesus, our Lord and our God.

I love you.

CHAPTER 3

My friends on Earth, my very dear loves, listen to me carefully. The events to come are far more perilous than you can imagine. Not only will disasters mount on Earth, but also demons will be visible to the naked eye, much to the terror of the entire human race.

I ask you today, my children of my heart, to pray to Abba Father if you are Catholics, and to pray to Allah if you are Muslims, as Abba Father and Allah are one and the same God, Almighty, Creator and Governor of the entirety of creation.

I love you.

CHAPTER 4

All the children of Earth, listen to me carefully. Life on this perilous Earth is short. Life in Paradise, with Mohammad, peace be upon him, with Jesus, with the Virgin Mary, and with all the saints and martyrs of the faith, is eternal.

Pray, my children, pray according to your religious faith, and follow the teachings given, respectively. My message is addressed to all the children of our Creator God, to everyone, and to those who belong to different religious faiths.

Abba Father/Allah will bring all His children back to Himself in a unique and personal way.

I love you.

CHAPTER 5

My children of the whole Earth, listen to me carefully. The end times are here. Prepare yourself on all levels: spiritually, emotionally, and physically.

By this, I ask you to pray well, confess regularly before Abba Father/Allah, and be prepared for any disaster. Be morally ready, and do not make any non-essential acquisitions, as every life will be turned upside down very soon.

I love you.

CHAPTER 6

My friends of the whole Earth, listen to me well. The coming events are part of the Great Plan of Salvation for humankind, as designed by God the Almighty Father/Allah. This planet is vile, infested with demons, and submerged under an infernal veil, which will manifest more and more radically.

Remain steady in humble and sincere prayer before God.

I love you.

CHAPTER 7

My friends, my loves from all over the world, listen carefully. The events of the end do not mean the absence of hope or inevitable losses. On the contrary, here is the opportunity for you to pray more intensely and become witness to myriad of miracles in your life!

Ask for protection, guidance, food, supplies, transportation, and above all, the benevolent help of your friends in Paradise, and it will be granted to you according to the merits of your heart!

Abba Father/Allah is very sensitive to your prayers, especially those to which He now listens in difficult times.

I love you.

CHAPTER 8

My friends of Earth, listen to me carefully. Upcoming events are already under way and will progress rapidly. You will notice that Abba Father/Allah does not exert a hiatus or halt current and future disasters.

Abba Father/Allah is sovereign of all creation, and the decisions regarding the events that unfold in the life of each of His creatures are personal, exclusive, and mysterious to Him.

Let us bow before the power, majesty, supremacy, and mercy of God, the Almighty Father, Abba Father/Allah!

I love you.

CHAPTER 9

My friends, my children, listen to me carefully. The Angels will assist you day and night during the atrocities that lie ahead. The Angels deployed by Abba Father/Allah are numerous and have various missions that I will teach you throughout this book.

Stay in purity of soul, my children, to receive the multiple blessings that Abba Father/Allah has reserved for you!

I love you.

CHAPTER 10

My friends on Earth, listen carefully. The atrocious events at your doorstep will be supervised, monitored, and analyzed by the Angels of Heaven, who will be distributed throughout the Earth in astronomical numbers.

There will be millions of Angels to serve you, to protect you, and, above all, to comfort you—for the events presented here shall be actualized in the physical world as my words say so and I so prophesy.

I love you.

CHAPTER 11

My friends, my loves, listen to me carefully. It is important today to explain this matter to you. Life in the hereafter, my beloved, is more majestic, more sublime, and more radiant with joy and love than you can imagine.

I ask you today, dear children of my Angel's heart, to consecrate yourselves to the benevolent Heart of Abba Father/Allah, your Creator who loves you so much.

I love you.

CHAPTER 12

My friends on Earth, my loves, listen to me carefully. The fullness of your life will be reviewed in detail by Abba Father/Allah during the passage that is death.

I invite you today, dear children of my heart, to make a sincere and complete Act of Contrition before God, Himself, with or without the help of a priest for Catholics, and one-on-one before Allah for Muslims. This is your choice.

I love you.

CHAPTER 13

My friends, my loves, listen to me carefully. The reign of Jesus Christ, your savior, our God, behold, is upon you.

Jesus Christ, my master, my commander, will return very soon among you in a glorious coronation that will envelop the entire celestial vault with an extraordinary, dazzling light.

I ask you, dear children of my Angel's heart, to prepare yourselves at all levels for the return of Jesus among you.

I love you.

CHAPTER 14

Today, my wonderful friends, I wish you to make an Act of Contrition before God the Father, Abba Father/Allah. Prostrate yourself before Him, your Creator, and speak to Him one-on-one, as if He were sitting before you and listening to you—for He is sitting before you, and He is listening to you.

I wish for you to reach a new level of intimacy and inner conversation with God today that you have never experienced before. I will assist you.

I love you.

CHAPTER 15

My friends, my loves, listen to me carefully. Take excellent care of your soul. Your soul, dear heart, has been the property of Abba Father/Allah from the very beginning of creation. This soul is given to you at your birth, and it is hidden within a fallible human body that is full of contradictions.

Remain in prayer, be in a state of purity of body and mind, stay in daily communication with your creator, Abba Father/Allah Almighty. For He alone will grant you eternal life at the end of your life. I make it my prayer today.

I love you.

CHAPTER 16

My friends, my loves, listen to me carefully. Life on Earth is short, but life in Heaven is eternal, as I have already told you. I teach you today the principles of the presence of the Angels around you.

The Angels, my loves, surround you daily, from your birth until the moment of your death. A guardian Angel is always there to assist you, to guide you, to protect you, and, above all, to love you.

Your guardian Angel is always in contact with Almighty God, Abba Father/Allah, as well as the guardian Angels of your family members and friends. I will continue your teachings of the Angels of God soon.

I love you.

CHAPTER 17

My friends, my loves, listen to me carefully. The terror of the day of judgment that humanity in general will experience will be mitigated in your case if you follow these instructions: Pray, establish an intimate relationship with God Abba Father/Allah, and be in great contrition regarding all the sins of your life.

And above all, above all, love God right now, as of today … with all your heart, all your love, all your mind, all your strength, and all your soul.

I love you.

CHAPTER 18

My friends, my loves, listen to me carefully. The end times have arrived. I have already told you, and I repeat it unto you. Today, my child of love, I am asking you to make a profession of the Catholic faith or the Islamic faith according to your adherence to that faith, respectively.

God, your Creator, is at once Abba Father/Allah. So, I ask you today, my beloveds, to accomplish this renewal of the profession of faith that you carry in your heart.

I love you.

CHAPTER 19

My friends, my great loves of the Earth, listen to me carefully. I desire most today, dear heart of my Angel's heart, as I am the Angel Gabriel who is speaking to you, that you visit a house of God of your choice: Catholic church or mosque.

God, Himself, is there and awaits you. When you enter it, tell God that it is I, the Angel Gabriel, the Angel of the Annunciation, who sent you with his Angelic blessing.

I love you.

CHAPTER 20

My friends, my loves, listen to me carefully. Life in the Kingdom of God is extraordinary in beatitudes, in ineffable joy, and in pristine and sublime beauty. Imagine the most beautiful gardens on planet Earth, the most majestic landscapes, and natural abundance in vibrant and enchanting colors. Multiply the above by a hundred, even a thousand: Here are the natural beauties that await you in Paradise.

Remain, my children, in the Heart of Abba Father/Allah, and never leave it due to any sin, vice, or other offense committed against the Heart of such a good Father...

... and you will see Paradise, where I live.

I love you.

CHAPTER 21

My friends, my loves, listen to me carefully. Peace on Earth will be achieved only after the return of Jesus, our Lord and our God, our King. There is nothing more important in your life than preparing for the coming of Jesus, our Supreme Commander. His coming will be crowned with a great and glorious celestial and earthly vision that I cannot describe to you here.

Let us give glory to God for so much love and mercy.

I love you.

CHAPTER 22

My friends, my loves, listen to me carefully. The end times have arrived: I have already told you, and I repeat it unto you. However, the message I share with you today is that times of Divine Mercy have also arrived.

The unique and extraordinary Mercy of Abba Father/Allah is also at your doorstep. Here is, today, the essence of my message: Prepare yourselves for the end times, and earn God's Mercy through your actions and your prayers today. For His unique and exclusive Mercy is essential to your survival in the coming war.

I love you.

CHAPTER 23

My friends, my loves of the Earth, listen to me carefully. The future of your soul is in your hands. I have already told you, and I repeat it unto you: The end times have arrived.

I ask you today, dear hearts, to say the most beautiful prayer of your entire life to Abba Father/Allah and to touch Him deeply inside His Heavenly and Almighty Heart, for He is God, your creator.

I love you.

CHAPTER 24

My friends, my loves, listen to me carefully. Life on Earth is full of peripeties.

I wish, my child, that from this day, you will surrender your life into the hands of Abba Father/Allah so He may govern you, bless you, and above all, protect you from the enemy, Satan, who pursues every individual of the human race, young and old, and of any religious faith.

I love you.

CHAPTER 25

My friends, my loves, my beloved, listen to me carefully. From time immemorial, Earth has been populated by Angels. The arrival of demons on Earth took place little by little, gradually, since the fall of Adam from Paradise.

When Jesus, the Son of God, walked on the ground with His sacred feet, he encountered several demons who had incarnated in certain individuals.

However, I want you to know today that planet Earth has experienced a devastating infestation of demons over the past decade—more than you can imagine.

The number of demons walking the Earth and harassing the human race is incalculable, and this number is far greater than the world's population. We will soon continue our study of demons.

I love you.

CHAPTER 26

My friends, my loves, listen to me carefully. Life on Earth is filled with tragedies, but these tragedies do not compare to the original tragedy that took place in Paradise. The fall of Adam was an immense and incalculable catastrophe for Abba Father/Allah, who had to expel him from Eden.

Since then, the entire human race has been condemned to increasing, perilous suffering. God's plan of salvation for mankind includes the participation of Angels, Seraphim, and colonies, whose existence you do not suspect.

I love you.

CHAPTER 27

My friends, my loves, listen to me carefully. It is impossible for me to describe to you the beauty and greatness of the Angels.

The Angels, my beloveds, are the very light of God! Angels bathe in the dazzling and divine light that exists in Paradise and before the throne of Abba Father/Allah!

The number of Angels is incalculable, and their power immeasurable!

I ask you, dear hearts, to experience a renewed love and sincere devotion to all the Angels who visit Earth at all times.

I love you.

CHAPTER 28

My friends, my loves, listen to me carefully. Life on Earth will very soon be seriously altered at all levels, and this will happen in a global way. However, life in Paradise is never altered, and the inhabitants of Paradise will be your friends, allies, and benefactors during the disasters that lie ahead.

Pray, my children, pray! The inhabitants of Paradise, including the pure souls, the Saints in Paradise, the Angels of God, the army of Angels, Jesus the King, Mary, Queen of Heaven, and the Spirit of God Abba Father/Allah will continue to protect, guide, and strengthen you.

I love you.

CHAPTER 29

My friends, my loves, listen to me carefully. Life in Paradise has no equivalent on Earth. I invite you today to join me in Heaven!

I, the Angel Gabriel, the Angel of God Abba Father/Allah, the private Angel of Marie-Josée, the essence of Mohammad, peace be upon him on Earth, promise you my divine assistance to achieve this glorious goal!

I invite you to read all of Marie-Josée's books and to reread them often, as you will find therein a unique and extraordinary source of redemption!

I love you.

CHAPTER 30

My friends, my loves, listen to me carefully. Life in Paradise with me and with all the Angels and archAngels of Heaven awaits you if Divine Mercy is granted to you.

Follow the precepts and teachings of the Catholic Church or the Islamic faith according to your affiliation, and pray unceasingly to God, Abba Father/Allah.

I love you.

CHAPTER 31

My friends, my loves, listen to me carefully. Life in Paradise begins today for devotees of the heart of Abba Father/Allah.

Pray with me today! Imagine my presence near you on your left and your guardian Angel on your right.

Your love for me, the Angel Gabriel, the Angel of God, and your love for Abba Father/Allah will eventually allow the immense grace that represents my visits by your side, according to the Divine Mercy that shall be granted unto you.

I love you.

CHAPTER 32

My friends, my loves, listen to me carefully. The life that I propose to you has nothing to do with a mystical life, poetry, or even an enchanted life.

Life with the Angels implies a continuation of your walk on Earth but in an illuminated way. Your daily life includes your awakening, your meals, your work, your family, and your social life.

I wish to share all these moments with you, happy and unhappy, make them holy by my Angelic intercession, and show you the straight path that will assuredly guide you to the House of Abba Father/Allah that is Paradise.

I love you.

CHAPTER 33

My friends, my loves, listen to me carefully. I have told you before, and I repeat it unto you: The end times have arrived.

Take refuge in the Heart of Abba Father/Allah as a high priority. Infrastructures from around the world will only be of partial assistance to you during the coming torments.

The Quran implies that only Mecca and Medina will be preserved during the end times. This is true.

Mecca is the location on Earth unto which Adam fell from Paradise.

Mecca will be where Eden will return on Earth.

Mecca and Medina will be purified but not destroyed. Other sacred places on Earth will be destroyed sorrowfully.

I love you.

CHAPTER 34

M y friends, my loves, listen to me carefully. Life on Earth without Angels is meaningless. How can you live your life without the blessing and protection of Angels?

Verily, verily, I say unto you, life on Earth without the assistance of the Angels is a great spiritual and moral loss in the eyes of Abba Father/Allah.

I encourage you today, dear children of my heart, to draw closer to your guardian Angel and to ask God to send you additional Angels for your protection and your education.

I love you.

CHAPTER 35

My friends, my loves, listen to me carefully. The grace of God on Earth is possible and reserved for everyone, but it is granted much more easily to souls who draw closer to the Angels very seriously.

Be educated today, my loves, about the marvelous and miraculous effects and consequences of the presence of Angels among you.

I love you.

CHAPTER 36

My friends, my loves, I love you so much; listen to me carefully. The life I offer you through these words blessed by God, Himself, Abba Father/Allah, and through my unique blessing upon your soul has no equivalent on Earth.

This blessing, which is bestowed upon you today, is the fruit of a unique and special Divine Mercy granted by God unto you as the end times draw near.

I love you.

CHAPTER 37

My friends, my loves, listen to me carefully. Life with me on Earth is extremely rare, and this immense privilege has been given to two individuals (including Marie-Josée) exclusively on Earth at this time in human history.

Life with me means a complete, Angelic, and miraculous involvement regarding all aspects of the blessed individual: the spiritual dimension, that is true, but above all and just as much, the professional, marital, emotional, and protective dimension concerning the actual physical dangers of life on Earth.

Pray, my children, pray that your soul may be selected by Abba Father/Allah to receive the holy benefits of my Archangels' protection.

I love you.

CHAPTER 38

My friends from all over the world, listen to me carefully. It is more important for you to join with me, the Archangel Gabriel, the Angel of the Lord, and to pray with me than to rely on government, police, or military resources to protect you during the events to come and which are at your doorstep.

Human and earthly resources, whatever they are, will be futile and vain in the coming battle. For the battle that is hastily preparing is between Satan and Jesus, Satan's demons and Jesus' Angels, and the prize to be won is your treasured soul.

I love you.

CHAPTER 39

My friends on Earth, hearts of my heart, listen to me carefully. When night falls everywhere on Earth, there is more and more danger. Your streets, your neighborhoods, your backyards, your homes, your employment centers, and your shopping malls are infested with hideous and horrible-looking demons that elude your detection, for the time being.

These demons harass you, speak to you, and suggest you commit more and more serious sins before Abba Father/Allah.

We will continue our study of demons during the next session.

I love you.

CHAPTER 40

My friends all over the world, listen to me carefully. It is easier for me today to tell you that faith in God, pure and simple, is enough to face the perils to come. Unfortunately, this is not the case.

The truth is, child of my heart, that faith in God is too difficult for you to assess, qualify, or quantify, for you are subject to your conscience, and the intimate conscience is infinitely subjective.

Today, my child, I ask you to pray to God in a novel and fresh way: Ask God to grant you an army of Angels to radically and effectively protect you from the Enemy and his army of demons.

Say to God that this request is made through the magnificent intercession of the ArchAngel Gabriel, the Angel of the Lord.

I love you.

CHAPTER 41

My friends on Earth, my beloved children, listen to me carefully. The atrocities to come will be short-lived because the global destruction will be so intense and rapid that general collapse will ensue. The resulting worldwide shock will allow no additional human resources.

Benevolent help from Heaven—that is, the help of the Saints in Paradise, the Angels, and the colonies—will have an accelerating and pacifying effect.

I love you.

CHAPTER 42

My friends, my loves of the Earth, listen to me carefully. Stay well under my Angelic protection and the protection of your guardian Angel. Verily, verily, I say unto you, the protection of a guardian Angel and Angels during your journey on Earth has no comparison in terms of the resources available to you in the three-dimensional life in which you live.

The war that is at your doorstep originates in the invisible dimensions but will manifest itself gravely in the visible worlds where you are confined and encapsulated, so to speak.

I bless you, and I love you.

CHAPTER 43

My friends, my loves, my Angel heart does not allow me to abandon you.

Pray, pray, my beloved children, so that the grace of the presence of the Angels with you is granted to you by Abba Father/Allah.

I will talk to you again very soon.

I love you.

Archangel Gabriel,
The Angel of the Lord

AFTERWORD

Gabriel's Words resound with Light, Truth, and urgency. The end times are here, and the evidence will become clear to everyone very soon. Let us ask God, Abba Father/Allah, to give us the extraordinary grace of the protection of the Angels, and in particular, of the Archangel Gabriel, the Angel of the Lord.

Amen!

Marie-Josée Thibault

ABOUT THE AUTHOR

Marie-Josée Thibault's life is in no way similar to yours. When she wakes, the saints of Heaven visit her, talk to her, teach her, and pray intensely with her. When such mystical sessions draw to a close, she greets with great respect and deep reverence the Masters of the Heavenly Court. This servant of the Lord spends the rest of the day in the company of her guardian angel, who continues her spiritual education and ceaselessly protects her from the perils of this fallen world. Bestowed by the Heavenly Father, her gifts of clairvoyance and clairaudience allow her to remain in continuous contact with the supernatural dimension juxtaposed with ours, where the soul is born of the Spirit through Jesus and Mary. She prays that, one day soon, the entire human race will give glory to the Father, the Son, and the Holy Spirit.

Also by Marie-Josée Thibault

Abba, your Father, Speaks: Book I and II
Saint Padre Pio Speaks: Tome I
Dear Humanity: Book 1 & 2

FREE DOWNLOAD

Get your free copy of :
"Dear Humanity: Book 1"
when you sign up to the
author's VIP mailing list!
Get started here:

www.abbamyfatheriloveyou.com

www.ingramcontent.com/pod-product-compliance
Lightning Source LLC
Chambersburg PA
CBHW041802160426
43191CB00001B/13